A Sorrowful Joy

Albert J. Raboteau

The Harold M. Wit Lectures
Harvard University
The Divinity School

Foreword by Kimberley C. Patton
Introduction by J. Bryan Hehir

PAULIST PRESS
New York, N.Y. • Mahwah, N.J.

Cover design by Lynn Else

Library of Congress Cataloging-in-Publication Data

Raboteau, Albert J.
    A sorrowful joy / Albert J. Raboteau ; introduction by J. Bryan Hehir ;
foreword by Kimberley C. Patton.
        p.   cm. — (The Harold M. Wit lectures)
    ISBN 0-8091-4093-4
    1. Raboteau, Albert J. 2. African Americans—Biography. 3. Orthodox
Eastern converts—United States—Biography. I. Title. II. Wit lectures.
BX739.R32 A3 2003
281.9′092—dc21

                                                                        2002003846

Published by Paulist Press
997 Macarthur Boulevard
Mahwah, New Jersey 07430 USA

www.paulistpress.com

Printed and bound in the
United States of America

THE HAROLD M. WIT LECTURES
Published by Paulist Press

Foreword

I arrived one spring evening last year to hear Albert Raboteau deliver the first of his two Wit Lectures on Living a Spiritual Life in the Contemporary Age, at Harvard Divinity School. I was startled to see that I had inadvertently left, in front of the Sperry Room speaker's podium, an Eastern Orthodox icon from a class on angels I had taught just a few hours before. The icon depicts the journey of the young man Tobias, as told in part of the biblical apocrypha, the Book of Tobit. Tobias is led firmly by the hand through the trials of land, sea, and air by the mighty archangel Raphael, whose name means "God heals." The winged angel, taller than his young charge, wears the expression of solemnity bordering on severity that is typical of Byzantine sacred art. That mood is somehow perfectly combined in the celestial face with the sweetest tenderness: the "sadly joyful" paradox that Raboteau finds in Eastern Orthodoxy, in African American spirituality, in life itself.

And so it was that this holy image "accidentally" emerged as a perfect commentary upon, and talisman of, the remarkable journey of the "soul in motion" we all heard that evening and the next. Just as clear as the fact that Albert Raboteau had traveled with courage and humility his unique path, combining as it did so many disparate identities, yearnings, and ideas in one personal history, was the fact that along the way he had been led by higher powers. "God heals" not only our deepest wounds, but then goes beyond mere restoration of whoever we were, whatever we have lost through sin and pain. Through the fires of suffering and of grace, if we will submit to them, God aims at nothing less than to transfigure us, allowing us to shine forth as who we were always meant to be. This soul-searing alchemy Orthodox mystical theology calls *theosis,* a radical term literally meaning "the process of becoming divine." It occurs through divine intervention, but just as surely through the vehicle of human compassion. Raboteau writes, "It is through us, if we permit it, that God reaches out to heal our wounds."

"So God created humankind in his image, in the image of God he created them; male and female he created them" (Gen 1:27). Perhaps no other description of the human condition carries with it such mystery and such responsibility as the biblical idea that every human being somehow bears the very image of the Creator *(tselem elohim).* The rabbinical and Kabbalistic traditions amplified this idea in countless ways. Perhaps the most striking is the extraordinary midrashic assertion that when any man walks down the street, angels go before him, crying out, "Make way! Make way for the image of God!" *(Tanchuma' Ekev 4).*

Patristic theologians such as St. Athanasius depended on this Genesis teaching in their insistence that since the divine image is original and latent in all of us, it can be restored to its full glory: "...He bestowed a grace which other creatures lacked—namely, the impress of His own Image, a share in the reasonable being of the very Word Himself, so that, reflecting Him and themselves becoming reasonable and expressing the Mind of God even as He does, though in limited degree, they might continue forever in the blessed and only true life of the saints in paradise" (*On the Incarnation* I: 3). The humanly realized divine image is then fully expressed in the incarnation of God in Jesus Christ, "the anointed one." The social implications are radical: injustice, degradation of the other, cruelty, or racism become impossible to justify. Every human being, through life's inevitable process of sin, confusion, suffering, repentance, forgiveness, purification, and redemption, has the potential from birth to become a unique and perfect mirror of the Holy One who is the source of all life.

What Albert Raboteau offers to those who read what is written here is the chance to reexperience that journey through its external events of both sadness and joy, as well as their deeper internal repercussions. Here in these lectures we find laid out, without self-defense, his spiritual autobiography. We travel with him, clutching the archangel's hand, his life overshadowed by the murder of his father at the hands of a white man before his birth, from a childhood spent largely in the North but rich in its French and African heritage in the deep South. We are steeped with him, through his family's generations of Roman Catholicism, in the rhythms of ritual, and in a sacramental view of the natural world, "the sensuous beauty of matter reflecting the glory of the spirit." We feel with him the travail of the civil rights and antiwar movements, the powerful influences of Dorothy Day and of Thomas Merton. We are led through his long, twisting road within academia, from Berkeley to doctoral work in the emerging black studies movement at Yale, to teaching appointments and academic distinction in his field at Yale, Berkeley, and Princeton. We plunge with him into perfectionism, alienation, over-extension, and struggle, into the degeneration and agonizing death of his marriage and the breakup of his family, into his loss of self and of loving communion with God, and the torment of his illness, guilt, and despair.

In the "joyful sadness" of the eyes of a Russian icon of the Mother of God, the *Theotokos*, Raboteau rediscovered ancient Christianity—and the road home—in the form of the Eastern Orthodox Church. Through conversations with a British monk and a fellow African-American historian, he began to recognize in Orthodoxy's embrace of suffering and redemption deep affinities to the piety of his ancestors: "…life in a minor key is life as it is….As the old slaves knew, suffering can't be evaded, it is a mark of the authenticity of faith." The discovery also offered theological confirmation of his insight, which had grown over years of study and reflection, that the bedrock experience of African slaves in America was part of a mighty river that stretched all the way back to the first few bloody centuries of the Christian Church. This was the tradition of the holy martyrs and confessors, marked by a powerful response to chronic and unholy suffering: the affirmation of faith, the insistence on divine regard, the transfiguration of the soul. This was *theosis*.

In an era where the language of "rights" and competing claims of victimization proliferate in every venue of our society, and particularly in the academy, Raboteau undertook a different interpretive trajectory. Perhaps no other contemporary scholar has with such unblinking vision realized the paradox of the African-American experience: it is a history not *only* of terrible injustice, not *only* of powerlessness and heart-searing wrong, but, just as importantly, it is *also* a chronicle of the ancient mystery of sanctification through the very instrument of suffering, the outrage of oppression. This application of the ancient Christian theology of the cross, whereby death itself is vanquished through the mystery of divine grace, is the story of the Resurrection. It does not deny the evil of slavery nor of the Crucifixion itself, but instead finds the light of bright victory in a narrative of what others have often represented as utter defeat.

Weakness becomes ultimate power; souls are forged and changed into gold. In Albert Raboteau's theology of African-American history, both before and after the end of slavery, countless "victims" are instead ennobled forever, wearing the crowns of the saints of old as they died in persecution, strong in their faith in God.

Thus he pursued his vocation in Eastern Christianity, knowing that the various streams of his identity had begun to converge. A month after the death of his beloved stepfather, surrounded by the "invisible cloud of witnesses," Raboteau was given the sacrament of chrismation at the Church of SS. Peter and Paul, a congregation just outside of Princeton descended from Russian immigrants. Chrismation is an ancient Christian rite of anointing with oil those seeking to be received as eucharistic communicants of the church. Its origins go back to the Davidic monarchy at the selection of a king, to the ordination of Aaronic priests, to the blessing of the appurtenances of the wilderness tabernacle and of the Jerusalem Temple. In the Eastern Church, not only adult catechumens but also newly-baptized infants are anointed, using oil blessed by the bishop, upon the head, ears, hands, and feet. Anointing, or unction, is also used in the sacrament of healing the sick, as well as at the final hour of human life. One begins and ends one's earthly life in the church anointed with oil, like a king, but also like the half-dead traveler upon whose wounds the Samaritan poured oil—sealed, healed of all sickness of body and soul, chosen and blessed forever.

The last step in painting an Orthodox icon is to rub it with warm oil: "[t]he oil serves to bind together the colors of the icon and to bring out their depth." Raboteau asked at the time of his chrismation, "Was that happening to me?" With the oil his variegated colors emerged, and the original stamp of God's image in him was revealed, just as Christ, the Anointed One, revealed God for the first time in earthly form. "'You cannot see My form,' the Scripture says," writes St. John of Damascus (*First Apology Against Those Who Attack the Divine Images*, 8). "What wisdom the Lawgiver has! How can the invisible be depicted? How does one picture the inconceivable? How can one draw what is limitless, immeasurable, infinite? How can a form be given to the formless? How does one paint the bodiless? How can you describe what is a mystery? It is obvious that when you contemplate God becoming man, then you may depict Him clothed in human form….When He who is bodiless and without form, immeasurable in the boundlessness of His own nature, existing in the form of God, emptied Himself and takes the form of a servant in substance and in stature and is found in a body of flesh, then you may draw His image and show it to anyone willing to gaze upon it…."

For Raboteau, the process of turning back to God and finding the self he had lost was not only about beauty, reconciliation, or ecstasy. It also demanded of him, as it does for anyone who dares to turn, the harrowing price of seeing his damaged life clearly in God's mirror. He was called to resolve lifelong griefs, first and foremost his father's mysterious death, but also those polar tensions that had previously threatened to tear him asunder—between monastic solitude and collective relationship, between the "holy" and the "ordinary." Repentance required of him the genuine seeking of forgiveness directly from those he had harmed.

Led as he was by the archangel into a new life (whose richness I will leave for the reader to discover), Albert Raboteau defies, transgresses, and thus ultimately transcends the rigid categories by which we so often judge and imprison one another in this country. His story carries with it the lesson that such transcendence is not only possible for each of us, but necessary. None of us is simply an aggregate of social, racial, or religious categories, or even of personal experiences. *None of us is only the sum of our wounds.* Each of us is as complex as he. To become truly oneself always involves painful self-confrontation, a kind of dread reckoning that can afford neither the blaming of others, no matter how cruelly benighted, nor the indictment of circumstances, no matter how unjust.

His journey shows that if the ordeal is accompanied by the willingness to accept at the same time the persistent workings of grace, the abundance of God's glory—of his particular love poured out for each one of us—then we can be lifted up on the great flood of his mercy. Our lives can be healed. Our faces, anointed as the royal, beloved children of the King, legitimate since the beginning of time when he first imagined us, can shine once again with Isaiah's "beauty for ashes, the oil of joy for mourning...."

Kimberley C. Patton
Harvard Divinity School
June 29, 2001
Feast of SS. Peter and Paul

Introduction

In February 2000, Professor Albert J. Raboteau of Princeton University visited Harvard Divinity School to give the Harold M. Wit Lectures on Living a Spiritual Life in the Contemporary Age. His words, delivered on two successive evenings, were extraordinary as he spoke them, and they retain their power here in published form.

Albert Jordy Raboteau, who is now the Henry W. Putnam Professor of Religion at Princeton, was born in 1943 in Bay St. Louis, Mississippi. In these pages, he gives such a dramatic account of his life that to go beyond what has already been alluded to in the Foreword would be to risk diluting the reader's anticipation. So, let me add only that his is a distinctly American story—a lyrical, particular comment on the assumptions of region, era, race, and religious tradition—but also a story that, through the discipline of personal reflection, and even confession, reaches into a place that knows no borders.

Al Raboteau has spent most of his professional career—as a scholar and teacher of the African-American religious experience and as an academic administrator—at Princeton and the University of California-Berkeley. But long ago, in the mid-1970s, he was a visiting lecturer at Harvard Divinity School. We are grateful that over the years he has maintained a close relationship with the School and its faculty and, of course, that he returned as the 2000 Wit Lecturer.

We at Harvard Divinity School are also grateful, always, to Harold Wit, a graduate of the College who established the lecture series in 1988 to bring to Harvard "unusual individuals who radiate in their thought, word, and being those spiritual qualities and values that have been so inspiring and encouraging to me along my path." And grateful as well to Paulist Press for once again bringing the testimony of one of those unusual people to a wider audience.

J. Bryan Hehir
Harvard Divinity School
Cambridge, Massachusetts
July 2001

Down Home

My grandfather sits in a chair placed outside in the light. He sits straight; his large hands push against his knees. The sunlight heightens the contrast between the stiff white collar of his shirt and the dark smooth skin of his face, turned in profile. He has sharp features, high cheekbones, and close-cropped hair. My grandfather was born in New Orleans, probably in the 1870s. His mother, Mary Lloyd, had been a slave; his father, Edward Ishem, was a German who sailed with the merchant marine. In the South they could not marry. When Edward Ishem decided to return to Germany with the boy, my great-grandmother, fearing she would never see him again, spirited her son away to a small town fifty miles east of New Orleans on the Gulf Coast of Mississippi named Bay St. Louis. There my grandfather, named Edward after his father, grew to manhood, became a carpenter and married my grandmother, Philomena Laneaux of St. James Parish, Louisiana.

My grandmother, of African, French, and Indian ancestry, faces the camera, her curly hair piled on top of her head. She wears a high-collar, Victorian-style dark dress. Her eyes are alert and bold. She gave birth to six children including my mother, whom they named

Mabel Sincere. She died when my mother was five and so my grandfather turned to his sister-in-law to help raise the children—a stern-faced woman with a down-turned lip, named Nanan Patience.

By the time I was born, my grandparents were dead. Their pictures hang on a wall in my house that I call my ancestor wall, and what I know of them comes from stories that I heard when I was young. When my mother spoke of that generation—"the old people," as she called them—she remembered them as proud, Creole-speaking, formal, and conscious of the distinctiveness of their mixed racial heritage, their language, and their religion.

There is another picture on my ancestor wall, a picture of my father, Albert Jordy Raboteau. He stands between my two sisters, a small, brown-skinned man with a mustache and a dapper-looking fedora. I never knew my father either. He was killed three months before I was born. He was shot and killed in Bay St. Louis, Mississippi, in 1943. He was shot and killed by a white man.

I was born into a family that was Roman Catholic as far back as we knew. I was baptized in St. Rose de Lima, a black church, and given the name Albert Jordy, after my dead father. When I was two, my mother, my sisters, and I moved to the North, partly because of what had happened to my father. The white man who killed him had claimed self-defense; there were no witnesses; the white man was not prosecuted. My mother decided that she did not want us to be raised in the South. So I grew up far away from my relatives, my extended family, but we returned during summers to visit relatives down home. One summer down South I remember especially well. I remember it as the summer of my education.

I remember the sea foam of the Bay, white against blue sky and dark water, the sea salt smell sharp in the humid air. We stop the car beside the beach; the hot sand burns my bare feet.

"Y'all can't swim theah, heah!" Two old white ladies sitting on their front porch: "Y'all can't swim theah!"

"Our little boy just wants to wet his feet in the water."

"Y'all can't swim theah; you go down to Waveland, the cullud beach at Waveland."

We get back in the car; we leave. My mother: "You damn cracker bitches, I hope to God your damn house blows down in the next hurricane." And it did. The power of a mother's curse that summer of my seventh year, summer South, down home.

That was after Birmingham, where it was hot. Heat from the pavement rises in dizzy waves when we go downtown shopping. Inside the department store, cool dark aisles, aisles of clothes to hide in. A woman's store; I'm bored. Over there, I see a water fountain, humming, metal, and shiny. I'm about to drink and I'm pulled back. "You can't drink there." "But I'm thirsty, Ma!" Then I see the sign, "For Whites." "Come with me." Down one aisle, around a corner, to a porcelain fountain "For Colored." I

15

drink tepid water. I feel my mother's fury. I drink; it is bitter. I feel her clenched rage.

From Birmingham we reached home, the Bay, where most of our people lived. Evening draws on. The air is thick with light and humid heat and the constant whine of cicadas. The houses smell of age and mildew. Old aunts, nanans, cousins, glazed with sweat and sweet dust of talcum below their necks where they clasp you and draw you close and speak their long-time love for you in words that sing with an accent like no other. We sit at the supper table eating, laughing, and listening to stories, stories about the old people, that go on late into the night. I hear about my great-grandmother, Mary Lloyd. They remembered her starching and ironing white shirtwaists while she sang snatches of opera she had heard in New Orleans. Her grandchildren used to laugh behind her back and call her Black Patty after a famous black operatic soprano of the turn of the century. Later, in the evening, I am sent to lie down on the couch to fall asleep. Their voices grow quieter, and they speak of things they didn't want me to know. Overheard whispers about my father's death, whispers about other dark, heavy, sad episodes threaded into my memory as I fell asleep.

Sunday morning we woke up late, too late for the last Mass at St. Rose de Lima. So we went to the white church, Our Lady of the Gulf, which my grandfather had helped build as a carpenter. Inside, white ushers direct us to sit in the back. We squeeze into a half pew with two other black worshipers. Two white men in front of us have a whole pew; they stretch out their arms on the back of their pew. Communion time comes. I go up and kneel at the rail. The priest, carrying the host, passes me by, and again passes me by, carrying the host in his hands, passing me by, until he had given communion to all the white people. I stumble back from communion, hot-faced with shame, a blur of numbness. Afterward, we drive away. I remain silent.

Forty years later, on a research trip to Charleston, I went to Mass in the cathedral in the old, historic district downtown. Late, I sit in back. At communion time, I rise to stand in line in a sea of white faces. I stand and I can't go, I can't go. I talk to myself, and turn to leave. I talk to myself and turn back to the line. I can't make myself go to the communion rail. I stumble out into the streets and I cry. A grown man with tears streaming down his face, tears that didn't fall that summer South down home.

Moving to the North, no doubt, helped our opportunities educationally and economically, but distance and time strained the ties of kinship with our relatives. I missed the rootedness and the community that I felt when we visited down home. In Bay St. Louis, unlike the North, there always seemed to be time enough for people to talk with one another. There was no rush with my relatives, as there was with the people up North.

They attended naturally to the daily tasks of community. Graciousness, gentleness, generosity, care, kindness, and politeness characterized my people. There was an ease about them which put others at ease, like a warm embrace. Being known because my grandparents and great-grandparents were known, I felt my place in a family that stretched back generations in the same place. Up North we had friends, but our trips down South taught me how much I missed the experience of extended familial community.

Nor did the North free us of the racial trauma of the South. My mother took a job as a domestic in a wealthy white household shortly after we moved North. One day, the children of the house had some playmates over and one of their little friends, a child of six or seven, called my mother a black nigger. My mother recalled with horror for years later how she threw the child to the ground and was about to step with her full weight onto his chest to crush him like a bug when something stopped her, some force, "my guardian angel," she claimed, and she came to herself. "Can you imagine what would have happened to me and to my children had I killed that boy?" I was fascinated and frightened by this story. Inchoately, I realized that we were surrounded by dangers that could strike at any time.

Life seemed precarious. We moved eight times in eleven years. We didn't have much. Though she tried to shield me from worry, I saw the sadness on my mother's face, due to the anxiety about where we would live next or how we would make it to the end of the month after the money had run out. Sometimes she sang religious songs to lighten her spirit or read a litany from her well-worn prayer book. When I tried to comfort her, she would smile and say: "Don't worry. God will protect us." Over the years, her strong faith in God's loving care seemed never to fail.

Our relative poverty had its lessons. I learned early to value simple things. When I was three and four, for example, I stayed during the day with an old woman named Stella, since my mother was at work and my sisters were in school. Stella had short steel-gray hair, and stubble for teeth, which made it difficult to understand her speech. She was poor and lived upstairs in an old rickety house, in a one-room apartment that always smelled of cooking grease. She liked chewing gum and we would share a stick whenever she had any. When she ran out, she would give me orange peels to chew on—"almost as good," she used to claim. Because we lived in rented rooms upstairs over someone else, I had to be quiet. My sisters were given the task of keeping me quiet in the afternoon by reading to me: comics, fairy tales, whatever, until they eventually grew tired, and so I learned to read by myself fairly early on—by the time I started kindergarten. I was a solitary child due to all that moving. I had few playmates. But being alone didn't bother me; I could read and use my imagination to make up games for myself. I enjoyed solitude.

When I was four, my mother married my stepfather, a man she had known down South. His name was Royal Woods, and I didn't think we needed him. It took me a long time to accept him and to understand his goodness and his love. He had been a priest, one of the early black priests trained in my hometown at St. Augustine's, a seminary founded in 1920 by the Society of the Divine Word to educate black men for the priesthood, because most seminaries would not accept them. He had known my family as a seminarian, and after his ordination he taught at the seminary. In fact, he was the priest who had baptized me. In 1947 he left the Society of the Divine Word and the priesthood. He left disillusioned and angry because of the racial prejudice he encountered in the church, even among fellow priests. Years later he would still get angry when he remembered the wrongs done to him and to other black priests, and the racism he saw in the American Catholic Church.

They got married and so were automatically excommunicated. They could not receive the sacraments. When we went to church every Sunday, I was aware of the pain they felt at not being able to receive communion. But one day they called me in to tell me that a dispensation had come from Rome that allowed them once again to receive the sacraments. They were very happy and so was I. I began to realize how important the church was with its sacramental life by seeing their pain at its denial and their joy at its restoration.

The church became more and more central to my life. I started Catholic school in first grade. Daily Mass attendance was mandatory, monitored by the sisters who taught all our classes. I sang in the choir, and started serving at the altar when I was ten. The sound of Latin, the glow of candles, the fragrance of incense, the splendor of the altar, the solemnity of the saints' statues—all surrounded me with sacred mystery. May processions, benedictions, Gregorian chant, the liturgy, the sacraments all supported within me a profound sense of the tangible presence of God. *Ad introibo ad altare Dei,* the priest would intone; *ad Deum qui laetificat juventutem meum,* I would reply. I decided that I wanted to be a priest. I wanted to stand at the altar and offer God in my hands. The progression of the liturgical seasons, Advent followed by Christmas, and Lent culminating in Easter, and fifty days later Pentecost, and then ordinary time. Ordinary time, even ordinary time was sacred. In sacred time events that transpired 2000 years ago lived on in the present, not just in memory, but in mystical reality. We lived these mysteries again and again, year in and year out. A regularity that offered stability in an impermanent world. Ritual seemed to draw aside the permeable veil between this world and the other world. I was enthralled with a sacramental view of life that meshed with my childhood experience of the natural world as an enchanted place.

We lived for several years on the edge of town in Ann Arbor, Michigan, close to a river and an island park. Behind our house stretched miles of fields, woods, and a creek, acres of room for a boy to wander with his dog. In those long ago summer days I rambled, totally at home, at peace and enraptured, taken out of myself by the sheer sensuous beauty, the overpowering smell of flowering lilacs, the last lingering light of sunset, the vibrant green of fully-leafed trees. I was lost in the moments of the day; running free—arrested by the shimmering light of the creek as it played across the rocks, or by the plunk of stones dropped into the surface of the pond. Nature was alive, pulsing with drama unexpectedly revealed: a broken bird's egg, a dead woodchuck, a fallen tree. My astonishment at the wondrous quality of the world; the intensity of smell, touch, sound, sight, and taste; the sheer beauty and poignancy of the world could break me into tears, because I knew it was all passing—all this beauty was passing. The lilacs would wither, the bits of shell would never yield a baby bird, the woodchuck's carcass swarmed with flies, the fallen tree stretched its roots forlornly to the sky. There was an edge of sadness to life that seemed as if it had always been there.

Not only in nature did I see death, for down-home relatives I knew began to die. Aunt Emily, my mother's favorite sister became terminally ill with cancer. We took the train south to see her before she died. She lived in the house where she and my mother had been born and raised, the large house of my grandfather Ishem. She lay in her bed and I remember her kindness as she called me over to give me her blessing. She seemed very holy. My cousin Johnny got hit by a car and died at the age of eleven. He lay in his coffin, the first dead person I'd seen. And then there was the death of my father. I began to accumulate pieces of the story from adult conversations: a grocery store, an icehouse, a fight, a shooting. What was back there in the past? Why did this absent presence continue to haunt our lives? Why didn't they want me to know what happened?

When I was thirteen I read a book that changed my life. It catalyzed unsettled movements of my spirit and gave them name and direction. The book was Thomas Merton's autobiography, *The Seven Storey Mountain:* The story of a sensitive, lost young man searching for his identity who converts to Catholicism and becomes a Trappist monk. Reading Merton shaped my conscious-ness of the spiritual life. His presentation of silence, solitude, contemplation, as the necessary conditions of the Christian life totally won me over. I wanted to be a monk. The monastic ideal had a long-lasting impact on my life. My solitary childhood resonated to the desire for solitude so lovingly depicted in Merton's text. The monk's life of simplicity and closeness to the land, his daily life of work and prayer echoing the cycle of the seasons, the clarity of the monk's purpose, *ora et labora,* pray and work, the sacralization of time effected by chanting the hours at set intervals of the day, the sober beauty of the Gregorian chant—all of this becomes a world of delight and consolation to my imagination.

I was good in my schoolwork. I worked very hard and my grades showed it. My academic success made my folks proud and fit my growing desire for perfection. I had assumed a heavy burden by the time I entered adolescence, a burden that weighed down my spirit. Already, as Mrs. Wheeler, my mother's close friend, recognized, I had become a "little old man." I did what others wanted of me and I did it well. After all, I was the favored child of the family, the only son. I bore my dead father's name and the family's future. I tried to become perfect. I prayed and worked. I wanted to be a saint.

At school, I was one of a handful of black students. I didn't talk about it, but I felt different and alone. The white kids were friendly at school, but we didn't visit one another's houses. Race was about to erupt into the national consciousness. In 1954 the Supreme Court in the Brown *v.* Board of Education decision declared separate but equal schools unconstitutional. The turmoil over the attempted integration of schools in Little Rock, Arkansas, captured national attention. My white piano teacher surprised me one day by apologizing for the behavior of white people in Little Rock. The murder of a fourteen-year-old black boy from Chicago in Mississippi, for speaking flippantly to a white woman, stirred the black community. Emmett Till had broken the racial code and stepped across a dangerous line and he paid for it. His body was found in a river and a grisly picture of his badly disfigured face flashed around the country. Till was only a little older than I was when two white men killed him. Then the Montgomery bus boycott of 1955 began something new—a movement. Black people became hopeful and determined to change the future. All of these momentous public events stirred in me a sense that we were living through important times. I went through adolescence and young adulthood during the civil rights era. My race was no longer just a family identity, it was cast against the backdrop of the historic role of my people, a destiny that involved "saving the soul of the nation." I realized these were historic times, the beginning of the death throes of an evil system that had shackled my people for so long.

In 1958, we moved to Pasadena, California, uprooting once again. Nature seemed despoiled, covered by concrete, ruined by smog. I no longer had time or place for solitary rambles. Everyone around me seemed too busy getting and going; too wrapped up in cars, the armor of daily struggle. I became insulated physically and emotionally from the natural environment. More and more I turned inward, away from the ugliness and impersonality of the environment. The monastic life seemed like an oasis in the desert. My parents enrolled me in an all-boys school, St. Francis, taught by Capuchin Franciscans from Ireland. Memorizing ten lines of Latin a night, I struggled at first to keep up, and then I found my balance and began again to excel in school. Unexpected winds of change began to blow in the Roman Catholic Church. A new pope, John XXIII, decided to call an ecumenical council, Vatican II. Within the next decade the Catholic Church I knew experienced a sea change. The ground was beginning to shift.

Besides preparing me to understand James Joyce, the friars taught me to love St. Francis of Assisi and his ideal of holy poverty. Under my clothes, I wore the scapular and cord of a member of the Third Order. In high school, I began to read a paper called *The Catholic Worker,* edited by Dorothy Day, a radical voice articulating Christian personalism, pacifism, voluntary poverty, and social justice. *The Catholic Worker* taught that it was not enough simply to discuss poverty or to write checks for the poor; you needed to have personal contact with poor people. Wealth was spiritually dangerous. We had lived on the edge of poverty; now I was learning the moral critique of our nation's drive for wealth and comfort. I became a fellow traveler of the Catholic Worker movement. In my senior year of high school I came close to filling out an application for admission to a Benedictine monastery, a small community devoted to common prayer and contemplation. But

I hesitated, figuring I needed more education and more maturity, since I was not yet seventeen. Besides, sexual awakening during adolescence led me to wonder whether celibacy was my vocation. So I went instead to college at Loyola, a Jesuit university in Los Angeles.

Before I left for college, my mother and stepfather sat me down to tell me the whole story of my father's death. There had been an argument between a black woman and a white man at the icehouse in the Bay. They began to fight. Nini, an older woman, and the sister of my mother's best friend, tried to stop the fight, and was threatened by the white man. When my father learned of this, he went to the house of the white owner of the icehouse to confront him. The owner wasn't home, but his wife was and she conveyed my father's anger to her husband. The next day, the white man came to the grocery store where my father was working as a clerk and shot him to death. The white man was arrested. He claimed self-defense; there were no witnesses and he was not prosecuted. My mother and stepfather explained they had not told me the story before because they did not want me to grow up hating white people. They wanted to shield me from the bitterness that corrodes the soul. I sat not knowing what to say. It was as if a secret was finally out and there it sat. I wasn't shocked, just confused about how to respond to this lifelong sadness. It would be years before I was able to come to terms with the death of my father.

So I went to Loyola, out near the ocean. I remember days of incredibly blue skies and dazzling light, moments of genuine excitement, intertwined with stretches of gray boredom and dull routine. I loved to roam the stacks of the library. Whole worlds of history, art, and literature lay open to my reach as I pulled books off the shelves that had nothing to do with any class assignment. And leafing through their pages, I traveled far in my imagination to different lands and times. I would just as soon have given free reign to the play of my curiosity, but our teachers insisted that we develop the skills of disciplined study: critical reflection, judgment, written and oral expression. At Loyola everyone took theology and philosophy every term. Too often this requirement meant courses on defending the Catholic faith, but occasionally its true purpose was served and the students caught a glimpse of "the perennial philosophy," as our teachers called it—a unity of vision in which our knowledge, our experience, fit into a pattern of meaning which we deeply desired but rarely had the perspective to see. At the core, tying everything together, we learned, was a simple and yet profound belief: the insatiable desire of the human spirit for knowledge is an expression of our profound yearning for the infinite reality of God. This ideal of education, as well as the dedication and integrity of many of my teachers, deeply impressed me and started me thinking about becoming a teacher, perhaps back home in the deep South.

The South was on everybody's mind in those years, as the civil rights movement mounted in intensity. The demonstrations in Albany, Birmingham, Washington, and Selma focused the attention of the nation upon the moral struggle of our times. When white police attacked unarmed black demonstrators with clubs, cattle prods, fire hoses, and police dogs in Birmingham, the face of racism stood revealed for everyone to see. We had seen it. Now white folks did, too. Martin Luther King, Jr., drawing upon the spiritual tradition of black suffering Christianity in his sermons and speeches, stirring old racial memories and deep religious emotions, thrilled my racial pride. Inspired by the civil rights movement and by voices in the Catholic Church that emphasized the importance of engagement with the world, I helped to start a tutorial program for grammar school children in Watts. Once a week, two carloads of Loyola students drove from campus to South Central Los Angeles to sit one on one with small black children who were reading several grades below grade level, if at all. I tutored a very shy and beautiful little girl. She was in third grade, but struggled with a picture book written for five- or six-year-olds. A year later, Watts erupted in flames in the worst race riot since the summer of 1943.

I continued to read *The Catholic Worker,* and I actually met Dorothy Day at a retreat in a Benedictine monastery in the desert east of Los Angeles. I remember being impressed with the strength of her personality and the radical implications of her words. Invited to address our group, she told us that it was morally necessary for the United States to disarm unilaterally. I was generally sympathetic with an antiwar position—I had been arguing against all comers in my freshman dorm that nuclear weapons made it impossible to justify any war—but her proposal seemed unthinkable. We were at the height of the Cold War! The retreat master attempted to settle our unease by saying he had no doubt that Dorothy Day would become a saint, but, if he were president, he wouldn't take her advice. I didn't think she could be dismissed so easily. In my college years, race and war dominated my sense of religious ethics as they would for years to come. Once again, the writings of Thomas Merton proved influential, as he turned from writing so-called "spiritual" books to books attacking head-on the issues of racism, materialism, and war.

By the time of graduation, I had abandoned the notion of becoming a monk or a priest. Instead, I decided to do graduate work in English literature, with vague plans of becoming a teacher. In the fall of 1964 I enrolled at Berkeley and fell headlong into the turmoil of the sixties. At Berkeley, the "movement" swept me, along with most of my contemporaries, to heady levels of idealism about social change and to stints of activism that interrupted academic business as usual. The next two years were a blur of political rallies, meetings, classes, and academic anxiety, as the free speech movement and the first Vietnam War protests pushed us out of the libraries and classrooms and onto the plazas and streets. For the first time in my life I fell behind in schoolwork and had academic problems.

My interest in studying literature dried up, as classes seemed to deal more with literary critics and criticism than with literature. Besides I fell in love, for the first time, with an art student from Canada. After she transferred to a design school back East, I moped around for months, finding it virtually impossible to study. I managed to escape from Berkeley with an MA in literature, but I didn't go off to teach. Instead, I felt the need to tend to inner business: I was beginning to doubt basic doctrines of Christian faith. So I decided, in the midst of all the inner and outer turmoil, to face my doubts by studying theology in a graduate program at Marquette University in Milwaukee.

Before beginning that program, I took a trip with my mother by train down home to see her closest friend, Nan Odette (Nini's sister), who had become senile. It was heartbreaking. This most gregarious and warm-hearted woman didn't recognize us. Occasionally moments of lucidity swept her mind and she would talk in the old way, but then they would pass and she would be gone. Like Nan Odette, the Bay St. Louis of my childhood memories seemed to be passing. The old ways were dying with the older generation. Many of the next generation had moved away, north or west, seeking jobs. I wondered whether there would be a down home to visit much longer. It was in fact my mother's last visit to her home of so many sad and joyful memories.

I went to study theology at Marquette. I also led, along with my two roommates, a student movement that shut the university down for two weeks one spring. We were determined to persuade Marquette to increase minority student enrollment and minority faculty recruitment on a campus that bordered Milwaukee's black community. We were also motivated by a nightly series of marches for open housing and the inner-city rioting that followed King's assassination. I found the power of the protest leader seductive. We spoke before crowds of enthusiastic students; our pictures appeared on the front pages of the newspaper; we were interviewed on radio; and the FBI established files on our activities. Meanwhile antiwar protests continued to escalate. We picketed, marched, organized rallies, and watched as the war also continued to escalate. We traveled to demonstrations in New York and Chicago. Despite all this activism, I went to class and passed my exams, but was turned down for the doctoral program. I applied for a position teaching theology at Xavier University, a black Catholic college in New Orleans, where my stepfather had once studied, and I was hired as a lecturer.

Teaching at Xavier was like going home for me. The Bay was only fifty miles away. I made several weekend trips to see relatives, especially my Nanan (godmother) Zenobia, my mom's older sister. I liked to ask her for stories about the old people, trying to piece out my family's background, especially on my father's side. One day she told me that she didn't know much about the history of the Raboteaus, but had heard that before the Civil War they owned members of their own family as slaves in northern Louisiana. When I pressed her for details, she said that's all she knew. Many years later I would learn that this story might hold the clue connecting my family ancestry to a French plantation owner in Haiti, and his origins in France.

I only taught at Xavier for a year, 1968–69, but it was a year of major transition. The national debate over Vietnam had become all-consuming. I decided that I opposed not only this particular war, but all war, and went through the lengthy process of filing for conscientious objector status. The ideas of Dorothy Day, Martin Luther King, and Thomas Merton figured prominently in my application. The assassinations of King and Robert Kennedy that year were followed by the accidental death of Thomas Merton in Bangkok. I mourned him as my spiritual father. The events and emotions of that year felt like one long letter, since I was corresponding almost daily with a young woman I had met and fallen in love with during my final months at Marquette. We courted through the mails until she found a teaching job in New Orleans.

Xavier confirmed my impression that teaching was to be my vocation. I loved it: the communication with the students, the excitement of ideas, struggling with issues of deep importance. Teaching theology, however, was leading me to lose my faith. I found that the academic study of theology, like the academic study of literature, removed me farther and farther from that which it studied. A career in teaching, I reasoned, would require me to get a PhD. Continued study in literature or in theology had no appeal for me. I wanted to study religion, especially the role of religion upon African-Americans' struggle for freedom, from a cultural and historical (rather than theological) perspective, so I applied to Yale, which had just begun a program in African-American Studies, and was accepted.

That summer I got married. The wedding was a huge Catholic service in a suburb of Chicago where my wife, Katherine, had grown up. My foster father was sick, so he didn't attend, but one of my sisters came, and my best man, Chuck, brought my mother, who was already showing signs of disorientation and memory loss from the arteriosclerosis that would kill her within a few years. After the wedding, my wife and I headed for New Haven to begin married life and, once again for me, a program of graduate study.

It was a heady time to be at Yale, which was at the center of the emerging black studies movement. That cultural movement set about to recover African-American history as a central part of American history. For many of us, the attempt to research and write about African-American history had more than academic significance. I felt that in the recovery of this history lay the restoration of my past, my self, my people. I chose to write about the history of the religious lives of slaves. As I sought sources for my work, I became fascinated by the voices of former slaves preserved in narrative accounts of their lives, not just as historical evidence but as voices that seemed to speak directly to me. These voices were special; they resonated with the wisdom that comes from those who have endured suffering and triumphed over it.

I was struck by the tenor of these voices, suffused with such sadness and yet juxtaposed with joy. I felt as if I were writing with eyes peering over my shoulders and voices whispering in my ears. What did they say, these voices? They spoke of human brutality, of whippings so severe that people died, of women miscarrying because of beatings they received, of fear by day and by night that they might be parted forever from those they loved. They spoke of cunning and secrecy, of coded messages, and forbidden meetings to praise God out from under the eyes of the master. They spoke with scorn of the white man's version of Christianity, which turned the religion of Jesus into a sham. They told of the dark, bloody history of this nation's past, of deeds so foul that "white people won't ever pray 'em away." They spoke of hope and Exodus, God's pledge that he would someday free his people, this darker Israel, from American bondage, as he had his chosen people of old. They spoke of closeness to Jesus, whose suffering their lives mirrored. Finally, they spoke of endurance and transcendence, the wisdom of people who were tried by fire and came out refined like gold. The depths of their faith condemned the emptiness of my own.

The wreckage of my faith had left me adrift. I had tried to construct a new faith for myself out of an aesthetic approach to life. What was important was beauty. To make beauty in your life was the only meaningful act. Life had no meaning beyond the fleeting moment of beauty. Then two events occurred that restored me to faith in God: the birth of my first child and the death of my mother. I could make no sense out of the depth and meaning of these events except through the sacraments. They were too profound for my aestheticism. Birth and death reached backward and forward in time, connecting us to communities past and to come. So we chose to baptize Albert Jordy (named after me and my father) in a small black Catholic church dedicated to St. Martin de Porres. The priest asked me to speak after the baptism and I was so moved I could barely get out the words, words that simply acknowledged what had already taken place—my son was now part of a community, an ancient family of living and dead that included him in its love and care.

Several months later my mother died in Pasadena. At her funeral the priest asked to read Psalm 23, "The Lord is my shepherd, there is nothing I shall want." Once again I felt the age-old words and gestures of the Christian liturgy holding us, caressing us, and helping us to heal. I was 3000 miles away when my mother died. I traveled to the funeral. My stepfather, my two sisters, and my best friend and his family were there, but it seemed as if we were exiles. This was not home; none of our relatives from the South were there. Mobility had stretched the ties of extended family to the breaking point. My mother was being buried among strangers. Death had found her wandering far from home. I clung to Paul, the two-year-old son of my best friend, at the gravesite. I needed to hold him. His stolid little body gave me strength and comfort, new life against the passing of the old.

With my mother's death, the last link to down home had broken. Or so I thought. But I was wrong. For there was so much that she and all those old people from Mississippi had bequeathed to me: memories, dreams, values, the acceptance of life's sad joyfulness, and deeper lessons yet to come.

Souls in Motion

Several months ago I was sitting at a table in Souls in Motion, a studio that's part of an outpatient clinic for mentally ill clients in central Harlem. I was listening to a client named James, who suffers severe depression. He tells me he feels like he is dying and worries that he's to blame. As we talk, Margaret, another client, approaches the table and sits down. She too is depressed. Her two young sons have just been adopted, which means that she won't have any contact with them until they are nineteen, and then, only if they decide to be in contact with her. Without a pause, James turns from his pain to comfort Margaret in hers. He consoles her, encourages her, and calms her. Once more I am amazed at the compassion of these wounded people, the love that shines in this basement room. How I got to be sitting there that day is the story of my own soul's motion, which I began to describe for you yesterday.

I started my teaching career at Yale, but moved back to Berkeley after two years, escaping the shadow of my mentors and the grayness of New Haven winters. I busied myself with establishing my career, preparing courses, revising my dissertation for publication, advising students, delivering papers at conferences. Our family grew. Albert was joined by two more children, Emily and Charles, born in California, and Martin, who came later. It was a busy time, full of pressure. I tried to make time for meditation and prayer each day. I began reciting the Psalms at set intervals in the morning, noon, evening, and night. We attended Mass regularly. As daily life got busier and busier, I craved silence and solitude more and more. Normally that would be a good spiritual impulse, but not entirely so in my case. My desire for solitude arose from something unresolved from my past, a lingering shadow vocation. It was my old desire to be a monk. The path not taken still haunted me. This romanticized image of the monastic life heightened my inevitable disappointment with the ordinariness of daily life. I felt that I had settled for second best, not the heroic, but the regular. I had chosen the lesser way.

Moreover, the incredible pressures of being a junior black faculty member at prestigious schools like Yale and Berkeley took its toll. I needed escape. I found it physically by running five or six miles a day in the hills behind campus and spiritually in pacing the old imaginary monastic cloister of my youth. Somehow, the monk had sneaked into marriage with me. Too often I became an absent presence as a husband and as a father. I was not fully there. I was distracted. Oh, I lived up to my obligations; I remained super responsible, but out of a sense of duty which I came to increasingly resent. If I had stopped to admit it, the obligations felt stifling, but how could I, trying to be perfect, admit that?

In addition to teaching, I got into part time administration, which ate up more of my time and my energy. My stepfather became ill and moved in with us until we found him room in an elder residence. All these pressures placed mounting strains on my marriage, but instead of facing them, I avoided them. Failure was too frightening to even consider.

The years drifted by. The children grew. I became more and more successful by the measures of academic success. Seeking a smaller and more personal teaching environment than Berkeley, I accepted an offer to teach at Princeton. Within a few years I was chairing my department and the old busyness continued unabated—more academic duties, more speaking engagements, more writing deadlines to meet. Time for solitude seemed to be time taken from my family. I felt vaguely guilty about everything.

I continued my religious practice—frequent Mass attendance, praying the psalms, meditation—but something seemed missing. The old pattern of perfectionism was proving too heavy a burden to bear. Responsibility upon responsibility, doing what other people wanted so habitually that it became difficult to even recognize what I wanted, was wearing me down. Finally the straw that broke the camel's back arrived in the form of an invitation to assume a major administrative office in the university as Dean of the Graduate School. A lot of people wanted me to say yes; it was prestigious, so I talked myself into it. I remember as I was driving to campus to accept the position, I physically felt that the street was narrowing, closing in on me. I shrugged off the sensation and took the job. It was "a disastrous success."

Sitting through meeting after meeting, from morning to after dark, I felt that my spirit was shriveling up and dying. Suddenly I realized why I had entered the academic life: to teach and to write. Now I was doing neither. Worst of all, the strain cracked apart my marriage. I rebelled. I became disastrously irresponsible. I had an affair. I left my wife, hurting her and my children deeply. I started an earthquake that only God could stop and the damage to several lives was devastating. It got so bad that every morning I would throw up. I couldn't stomach the mess I had made of my life. I kept up the daily schedule of appointments and tasks, but my spirit was bleeding all over the place. Bad as it was, other forces were stirring.

Early in that disastrous year, an exhibit of Russian icons had opened at the Princeton Art Museum. It was called "Gates of Mystery: The Sacred Art of Russia," and it simply astonished me. I went back three times. One icon in particular attracted me with its spiritual power, an icon of the *Theotokos* with sad loving eyes. She seemed to hold all the hurt in the world with those eyes. I stood in front of her for a long time. I gazed at her and she gazed at me. A few days later I met a man, named Jan, who had also seen the exhibit. It turned out that he was a recent convert to Eastern Orthodoxy. I mentioned that I had visited an Orthodox Church once in San Francisco and he invited me to attend a service at his church some Sunday. A few weeks later he picked me up and we drove twenty miles out of Princeton to SS. Peter and Paul Orthodox Church in Manville. My experience with the icons recurred; I was overwhelmed by the spiritual power of the Divine Liturgy, as the Orthodox call their service. I was moved especially by the hymns. They had that same sadly joyful tone which I associated with down home and with slave spirituals. I was surprised as well by the hospitality of the congregation after the service. Mostly second- and third-generation descendants of Russian immigrants, they welcomed me with ease. I kept going back to SS. Peter and Paul Sunday after Sunday. And as my life fell apart, I would stand in the church, emotionally shaken, and feel the prayers of the congregation as if they were so many hands holding me up. On the night of Pascha (Easter), we processed around the church with lit candles three times and then stopped at the doors of the church chanting "Christ is risen!" When the doors opened and we all moved into the church, I felt the presence of generations of Christians standing with us, generations moving into the church with us: martyrs, confessors, our ancestors in the faith. I put up an icon corner in my bedroom and prayed

42

before the icons by the light of an oil lamp that I kept lit against the darkness without and the darkness within. I hung the pictures of my relatives on a living room wall and looked to them for help and strength.

Half way through the year I resigned my administrative position to take effect in June. That summer I went to Europe ostensibly to participate in a conference, but actually searching for my lost self. On my way to the conference, I visited an Orthodox monastery in England, St. John the Baptist. I befriended one of the monks and told him about the disintegration of my life and my growing attraction to orthodoxy. He listened compassionately and remarked how similar my story was to his.

The daily office of the hours, the liturgy, and the afternoon recital of the Jesus prayer in Greek, English, and French, opened within me tears of repentance over what I had done. "Lord Jesus Christ, Son of God, have mercy upon me a sinner." I repeated the ancient prayer over and over and over. As I left, my monk friend said something that surprised me: "I've often thought how similar orthodoxy is to African-American spirituality." I traveled on to the conference in Austria, stopping at Florence and Assisi on the way. I prayed before the cross of San Damiano that long ago spoke to St. Francis, but it did not tell me what to do. I lectured at the conference and returned home knowing that my life had been overturned. I had failed the most important relationships of my life and I had done so in search of some spurious form of sanctity. By the time I got back home, I was sure I wanted to become Orthodox. It was not as if I had sat down and systematically searched for an alternative to Roman Catholicism. I had not set out to find another church. All of this was experiential. I was being led on a path unforeseen. I told only a few friends of this unusual development. One of them, a fellow historian of African-American religion, echoing the English monk, asked me if I understood how much orthodoxy fit the aspects of African-American religion that had most personally interested me over the years. I said no.

A month after my return, my foster father began to die. He had a stroke and was taken to the emergency room of the local hospital. I hurried to the hospital. There he lay, his face twisted, his body convulsing, and his breathing—aided by a tube inserted down his windpipe—came in gasps. The seizures wracked his whole body every five minutes. A nurse came in to check the respirator and spoke to him kindly. "How are you doing, Royal?" What had the stroke done to his mind? I wondered. That mind that used to love to read, to study Greek and Latin grammars, dictionaries, the latest translation of the Bible, after a long day of work as a janitor, the job he found in order to support a widow and her three children. Over the next two days I sat for hours at his bedside, watching him, waiting for him to die. I read him psalms aloud. I held his hands, the hands that had baptized me as an infant fifty years before. His lungs were so full of fluid, every breath was a gasp. Two aides came to bathe him; they talked to him and gently stripped him of his blanket and his gown; they bathed and powdered him, and dressed him again. I went out to get dinner and while I was gone he died. At his funeral Mass a priest from the Society of the Divine Word, who saw the obituary in the newspaper, arrived to concelebrate. The order remembered their absent brother Royal at the end. The evening of his burial, I sat alone, reflecting: My mother is dead; my two fathers are dead; no generation stands between me and death. Lord have mercy upon us.

A month after my foster father's death, I decided to speak with Father James, the pastor of SS. Peter and Paul, about entering the church, and we held several conversations to make sure I was prepared. Then one Sunday in December, at the start of a very bleak winter, I stood in front of the congregation, with Margery and Timmy, the wife and son of Jan, the man who had first invited me to his, now our, church, to receive the sacrament of chrismation. The priest anointed my head, eyes, nostrils, ears, lips, chest, hands, and feet with holy oil and gave me a lit candle to hold as I stood for Divine Liturgy. The anointing made me recall the last step in the process of icon painting, which is the application of warm oil. The oil serves to bind together the colors of the icon and to bring out their depth. Was that happening to

45

me? At the start of the liturgy we sang the words of Psalm 103: "Bless the Lord, O my soul, and all that is within me bless his holy name." And I was moved again by the sad joyfulness of the chant tones. I took as my chrismation name Panteleimon, after an early Christian martyr and healer. The name means *the all merciful*. Mercy upon mercy, like healing oil, had been poured out on me.

Free of administrative duties for the first time in six years, I returned to teaching with relief and excitement. I felt I needed to teach in a new way, so I designed some new courses and chose small seminars over large lecture courses. My writing took on a different direction and a different voice, more personal, more directly religious. I began to take keeping a journal more seriously and began to see writing itself as a spiritual discipline, a form of waiting expectantly for mystery to be revealed. The different areas of my life seemed to be coming together. Suddenly I felt that I needed to go back to Mississippi, to the Bay, to research the story of my father's death. I thought of it initially as a historical project and I took along a video camera to record interviews with my relatives and to capture images of the town. I didn't know what I would find after all these years, but I needed to go. Down home I talked to aunts and uncles, cousins, and close family friends about their memories of what had happened in that summer of 1943. I found two newspaper accounts of the shooting of my father. I found out the name of the man who shot him—Summeral. I went to oasis in the desert. My parents enrolled me in an all-boys school, St. Francis, taught by Capuchin Franciscans from Ireland. Memorizing ten lines of Latin a night, I struggled at first to keep up, and then I found my balance and began again to excel in school. Unexpected winds of change began to blow in the Roman Catholic Church. A new pope, John XXIII, decided to call an ecumenical council, Vatican II. Within the next decade the Catholic Church I knew experienced a sea change. The ground was beginning to shift.

Besides preparing me to understand James Joyce, the friars taught me to love St. Francis of Assisi and his ideal of holy poverty. Under my clothes, I wore the scapular and cord of a member of the Third Order. In high school, I began to read a paper called *The Catholic Worker*, edited by Dorothy Day, a radical voice articulating Christian personalism, pacifism, voluntary poverty, and social justice. *The Catholic Worker* taught that it was not enough simply to discuss poverty or to write checks for the poor; you needed to have personal contact with poor people. Wealth was spiritually dangerous. We had lived on the edge of poverty; now I was learning the moral critique of our nation's drive for wealth and comfort. I became a fellow traveler of the Catholic Worker movement. In my senior year of high school I came close to filling out an application for admission to a Benedictine monastery, a small community devoted to common prayer and contemplation. But fourteen-year-old black boy from Chicago in Mississippi, for speaking flippantly to a white woman, stirred the black community. Emmett Till had broken the racial code and stepped across a dangerous line and he paid for it. His body was found in a river and a grisly picture of his badly disfigured face flashed around the country. Till was only a little older than I was when two white men killed him. Then the Montgomery bus boycott of 1955 began something new—a movement. Black people became hopeful and determined to change the future. All of these momentous public events stirred in me a sense that we were living through important times. I went through adolescence and young adulthood during the civil rights era. My race was no longer just a family identity, it was cast against the backdrop of the historic role of my people, a destiny that involved "saving the soul of the nation." I realized these were historic times, the beginning of the death throes of an evil system that had shackled my people for so long.

In 1958, we moved to Pasadena, California, uprooting once again. Nature seemed despoiled, covered by concrete, ruined by smog. I no longer had time or place for solitary rambles. Everyone around me seemed too busy getting and going; too wrapped up in cars, the armor of daily struggle. I became insulated physically and emotionally from the natural environment. More and more I turned inward, away from the ugliness and impersonality of the environment. The monastic life seemed like an the courthouse to find the arrest record and to the police station to see if I could locate the arresting officer's report. I was told that the old reports were somewhere in storage, but one of the officers remembered that Summeral had a son who practiced law in a nearby town. I located his number and called him on the phone to ask him if he knew anything about my father's death. He said that he was nine years old at the time and remembered my father well. His family's version was that my father had threatened his father, then physically assaulted him, and his father fired a gun in self-defense. I asked what had happened to his father and he said that in later years his father had developed terminal cancer. After a pause, he added that his father had shot and killed himself. We agreed that someday we would meet. On the last day of my trip, I went to visit my father's grave. I had been there several times before. My mother had taken me the first time when I was a few weeks old and every time we came to the South, we had gone to the grave to pay our respects. But this time was different. I looked at his grave and I began crying. I cried for him, for my mother, for my sisters, for a father and son who never met. Then, as if in memory, I saw him. I saw him laughing; I saw him angry; I saw him shot and falling, falling into my arms, into my life. After all these years of waiting, my father and I had finally met. I bent down, picked up some dirt from his grave and rubbed it on my head. All the sorrow welled up inside me and merged with the joy of meeting him finally for the first time.

◻

That spring I took the train into New York and traveled up to Harlem to see an exhibit of Ethiopian icons at the Schomburg Library and Museum. Very different in style from the Russian icons I had begun to learn to "write," the African Zion exhibit, as it was called, graphically reminded everyone who saw it of how ancient Christianity was in Africa. I was excited to see an African face of orthodoxy. I told people at my church about the exhibit and also arranged to meet a friend in New York to see it again. She suggested that I meet her at a place called Souls in Motion on 127th Street near Lenox Avenue only a few blocks from the Schomburg. She said she had to visit some people there and then we would go see the exhibit. As it happened, I got there before she did and found a room full of people who were sitting reading the Delaney sisters' book, *Having Our Say.* The two women leading the reading beckoned me into the room and introduced themselves as Julia and Louise. I learned that Julia had founded Souls in Motion as a studio to encourage mentally-ill clients to express their creativity through painting, sewing, drama, cooking, writing, or music. Moreover, "the room," as the studio was called, served as a place of hospitality, a space where people could talk and be listened to with respect and compassion. Souls in Motion, under Julia and Louise's guidance, had developed into an amazing community of caring, attentive, sensitive people. I liked what I saw very much. I met several clients and talked with them—James, and Ethel, and William. I never got to the exhibit. A few weeks later, I visited Souls again, and then again. Julia and I began to date, and after a while dating turned into courting. As I visited the room more frequently, I was struck by the spirituality of the clients. How frequently they spoke of God and their gratitude to God for what they had and for his bringing them this far. They extemporized wonderful, moving prayers for friends and clients who were sick, or hospitalized, or in difficulty. Despite their own troubles, they expressed their concern for each other and for my children and me. Julia asked me to teach a writing seminar for the clients once a week and it is still going after five years.

As Julia and I continued to court, she learned more and more about orthodoxy, experientially, by attending Divine Liturgy. She had already come to appreciate the deep faith of the clients she worked with in Souls in Motion. It was no accident that she settled on that name for the studio. We visited a wonderful interracial Orthodox community in Kansas City, Missouri, dedicated to St. Mary of Egypt. Located in the heart of the inner city, this community had worked with drug addicts, alcoholics, battered women, and the poor, and had developed a special outreach to African-Americans. Every year for seven years it has sponsored a conference on Orthodoxy and African-Americans. At three of the conferences I spoke and in my talks had a chance to reflect on the cryptic comments of my friends, the monk, and the historian, about the affinities between orthodoxy, African-American spirituality, and my own religious bent. I have already mentioned the quality of sad joyfulness, a sense that life in a minor key is life as it is. Christianity is a religion of suffering. The suffering of Christ and of the martyrs is at the center of the Christian tradition and suffering grounds the Christian to the suffering of the world. As the old slaves knew, suffering can't be evaded, it is a mark of the authenticity of faith. The primary example of suffering Christianity in this country was the experience of African-American slaves. Both viewed the person as embodied spirit and inspirited body. Both understood matter and spirit to be related, not antithetical. Hence the use of material and bodily gesture to reveal the presence of the spiritual to our bodily eyes. Both held a profound trust in the healing power of ritual. Ritual in both spiritualities opens the door to the other world. Both understood being as communion: a web of relationships stretching into the past and the future constitutes the person. Both criticize individual aggrandizement as destructive of the person. The good and wise that have died continue to act in the present to protect and guide those who ask for assistance. It seemed to me as if all the religious tendencies and sensibilities of my childhood—the love of the liturgy, the sacramental vision of the world tied to the beauty of nature, the sacralization of time in the liturgical seasons, the sensuous beauty of matter reflecting the glory of spirit, the living connection of my person to those who had gone before, the refusal of my people to let injustice strike down their souls and demean their human dignity, the old people's example of gentleness, hospitality, and kindness—all of these qualities, my legacy from childhood and beyond, seemed now to be confirmed, renewed, and fulfilled in the merciful oil of chrismation, binding together my colors and bringing out their depth.

My youngest son, Martin, started attending church with Julia and me, and soon became chrismated too. After an amazing encounter with St. Elizabeth of Moscow, Julia was chrismated, taking the religious name of Elizabeth. Within the year we married in an Orthodox service held at Columbia University chapel, close to Harlem, so the community from Souls in Motion could attend. A busload of parishioners also came from our church in Manville and the reception was held in the basement room of Souls in Motion. For an afternoon, at least, two distant communities were brought together, to celebrate the wedding of a couple that belonged to both. A harbinger of things to come.

How to integrate the disparate communities of my life: black and white, inner city and suburb, religious and academic? How to integrate the disparate impulses within myself: solitude and community, spirituality and scholarship, silence and speech? These were the spiritual questions that now came to the fore. One night I had a vivid dream that seemed to speak about these issues. I dreamt that I was standing with Julia on the northeast coast of England facing an island. Our access to the island depended on the tide, which had receded, allowing us to walk across by stepping on a series of wooden pylons and rocks. Beyond the island lay another, much smaller one, which I realized was "my island." The larger island was deserted and treeless but the land glowed with a yellow-green color. I knew that if we could find the door, we would discover the entrance to an underground cloister of an ancient monastery.

Several days later I told this dream to a friend, who said, "There is such a place. It's called Lindisfarne." I had not heard about Lindisfarne, other than the Lindisfarne gospels, but my dream accurately depicted it, as I learned later—a tidal island, with another smaller island lying off its southern coast like "my island," almost exactly as I dreamed it. A year later, Julia and I took a trip—for me, a pilgrimage—to Lindisfarne. When we arrived, I was disappointed at the tourism and development of "Holy Island," as it's known. What drew my eye was the small island off the coast which I took to be the same small island of my dream and which is known as St. Cuthbert's Island, the site of the saint's hermitage.

Cuthbert, one of the most popular saints of England, was a seventh-century monk who became prior of the Lindisfarne monastery. He was widely known for preaching to the surrounding people and for working miracles far and wide. After he served as prior for several years, he retired to the stone hermitage he built on the small island close to Lindisfarne. But his solitude was constantly broken by a steady traffic of visitors seeking advice and blessings. So he moved to Inner Farne, an island seven miles further out into the Atlantic. Then he was chosen bishop. He refused the office, but finally yielded reluctantly to the repeated requests of the king and clergy. After two years, sensing his impending death, he resigned and returned to Inner Farne, where he died. The monks buried his body at Lindisfarne, but then removed it because of Viking raids and, after years of wandering, the saint's remains ended up in Durham. A cathedral was built over his tomb.

When we saw Cuthbert's Island, "my island," I felt strongly that this was the goal of my pilgrimage and that this was, for me, the holy place—not Cuthbert's tomb in Durham Cathedral and not Lindisfarne itself. It was this small rocky place that I felt I needed to reach. The tide, however, wasn't yet fully out, so it was impossible to walk to the isle without wading in cold North

Atlantic seawater. After a few minutes of hesitation, I decided I didn't care; I had to get there any way I could so I began to walk over, stepping slowly on the wet rocks, seaweed, and mud. Julia followed. Once on the isle, she considerately wandered off to give me space to be alone. I walked out to an edge of rock that faced toward the sea and sat down. This was indeed an "absolute" place, a place to encounter the awesome presence of God. I felt for a few moments a sense of being alone and at peace with the rocks, the sea, and the gulls skimming the sunlit water, the shimmering waves, and the low gray clouds. I thought of how cold and stormy it must be in wintertime. Behind me, the ruins of a stone chapel encircled a tall wooden cross and I wondered what it would have been like to dwell there in a cell of rock. Here was my old childhood monastic ideal in all its stark beauty—my island.

Suddenly my solitude was broken by a woman walking nearby. I was upset by the interruption. (This was *my* island.) Gradually, by twos and threes a group assembled, perhaps twelve people in all, sitting on the circle of stones where Cuthbert's hermitage had once stood. It was a group of pilgrims on retreat at Lindisfarne, and they asked if we would like to join them in prayer. One by one they began to read prayers from Celtic prayer books. They read slowly and meditatively. Then it came my turn. "Dear God, thank you for the beauty of this day and the wonderful providence of our fellowship. Thank you for bringing us together from such far distances, over so many miles to this place that is suffused with the holiness of your saint. Preserve us so that we may take with us some of the holiness we feel here. Thank you for your love which sustains us at each moment and each breath." As we continued to pray around the circle, I wondered at the tangible, gratuitous love that had brought us all to Cuthbert's Island.

As I reflected on the trip and the dream that lay behind it, I thought about what I knew of Cuthbert's life and what it might mean for mine. I began to understand the connection between solitude and community. They aren't antithetical but contrapuntal. How mistaken I had been to identify monastic solitude as the place of holiness, and community as the place of ordinary humdrum responsibility. The ordinary is holy. I understood that it was possible, no necessary, for me to make peace with the desire for solitude and the burden of responsibility. To live the antinomy of solitude and community was my calling. I would meet Cuthbert again.

One Sunday at coffee hour after Divine Liturgy in Manville, two of the other church members and I began to talk about the need for an Orthodox parish in Princeton. One of them said, "I know just the place. There's an empty church that a Catholic parish outgrew." I knew the church—a small, white, wooden frame church that I had passed and even stopped to look at once or twice. We organized a general meeting and within a few months received permission to start a mission. The Catholic parish agreed to rent us the little church and we held our first liturgy there two years ago this March. We started with perhaps ten members and have grown steadily, though our membership is still small. We chose to dedicate the mission to the Mother of God, "Joy of All Who Sorrow," as a sign of our desire to minister to those who suffer and are in need. We sing her hymn frequently in the services:

Joy of all who sorrow art thou,
And protectress of the oppressed,
Feeder of the hungry,
Consolation of travelers,
Haven for the tempest tossed,
Visitation of the sick,
Protection and aid of the infirm,
Staff of old age,
O, all pure Mother of the Most High God,
Hasten, we pray, to save thy servants.

(My mother would love that hymn.) From the start, I have been the lay coordinator of the mission, responsible for organizing the week by week and day to day details of the growing community. Our small size brings a sense of intimacy, as well as the usual tensions that exacerbate personality conflicts. On the first Sunday of Great Lent, Forgiveness Sunday, we observe a ceremony after Vespers in which each person bows deeply to every other person in the community and asks each of them to "forgive me a sinner." The response is "God forgives; forgive me a sinner." When I start worrying too much about whether we will succeed, I remind myself it is all in God's hands. But I keep worrying. The tension between responsibility and detachment is still taut within me. Julia and I have started to invite clients from Souls in Motion to spend time with us at Princeton and to visit the mission, if they desire; and we have invited members of the Joy of All Who Sorrow mission to come to visit Souls in Motion as well. We intuit that bringing these two communities together is a vital part of our mission. I remember *Howard Thurman* and his profound search for interracial community. Soon he joins Merton and King on my picture wall.

Realizing the incompleteness of my repentance, I visited my former wife and asked her forgiveness for my responsibility for the death of our marriage. She says she forgives me and asks my forgiveness for her part in the death of our marriage—our personal forgiveness Vespers.

Two years after the pilgrimage to Lindisfarne, Julia and I went back to England. This time we went to St. John the Baptist, the Orthodox monastery in Essex that I had visited alone four years earlier, during my time of darkness. The monk I had befriended was still there. He asked what had happened since he saw me last. I told him that I had gone through a painful divorce, had become Orthodox, and had remarried. I told him of the new mission that Julia and I had helped to start and asked for his prayers. In our conversation I mentioned the trip to Lindisfarne and my connection to Cuthbert, and his eyes lit up with mischief. He said, "Just think of it. That huge cathedral in Durham is built on the relics of that one man." Then he told me the story about St. Cuthbert's body being exhumed in the nineteenth century and how an Anglican rector had taken some relics of Cuthbert and that some of them had wound up in his hands. He asked if I would like a relic of the saint. The next day he handed me a small silver reliquary cross containing a relic of Cuthbert. Immediately I hung it around my neck.

On the last day of our visit to the monastery, Divine Liturgy was crowded with Sunday visitors from London. A woman pushed her paralyzed son forward through the crowd in his wheelchair to receive holy communion. I wished that I could touch the boy with the relic and that once again St. Cuthbert would heal him as he had healed many of old. I didn't, but I felt the compassion, the desire to heal that not only I but also all those around me felt for this boy and his mother. I realized it was a very old feeling and suddenly, it was transformed into an overwhelming apprehension of how much God loves all of us, each of us, at every instant, and that it was God's love, certainly not our perfection, that matters.

What I perceived then, I realize now, was the very same compassion that I had seen in the eyes of the *Theotokos* in the icon exhibit. It was the same love that Joy of All Who Sorrow represents to the members of our small mission. It was the selfsame compassion that moved James to comfort Margaret that day in Souls in Motion all the while he was suffering. It was the same love that spoke in the warm embrace of my people down home. It was the same love that prompted my stepfather and my mother to console each other in their grief and disarm their anger. I realize now that all my life a community of love has surrounded me, even when I did not see it. How often we don't see the moments of love. The pain, the injustice, the abuse, and the evil—passing on generation after generation—blind us. But if we search, we can see that our compassion conveys God's love. It is through us, if we permit it, that God reaches out to heal our wounds. And it is through our love for one another that he transforms our sadness into joy.

On the day we left the monastery I looked for my friend to say goodbye, but I couldn't find him. On the train to London, I found a small red box in my briefcase and asked Julia if it was hers. No, she replied. I opened it and there was a replica of Cuthbert's pectoral cross. My friend had sneaked it into my bag.

Back home, I return to ordinary time. Our mission continues to grow. Problems break out: some heal, some fester. I teach my classes—a seminar on religious radicals in which we read Day, King, Merton, and Thurman, among others; a seminar on Merton with five students; a class on the spiritual classics of Eastern and Western Christianity; as well as my course on African-American religious history. I walk by the lake with my dog every day, and sometimes we glimpse a great blue heron. Startled, it spreads its huge wings and flies off over the lake, squawking in indignation at our disturbing its peace. Julia and I drive to the train station for her morning commute into the city. Sleepily we recite the Trisagion prayer—"Holy God, Holy Mighty, Holy Immortal, have mercy on us"—and ask God to bless our day. Once a week I travel to New York to teach my writing class to the clients at Souls in Motion. They continually surprise me with their gratitude, their kindness, and their utter trust in God. Cordelia consoles Jerry who feels lonely. Lorna consoles Ethel whose daughter has run away from home. They teach me. Grace is everywhere.